Romancing On The Rock

A Man's Guide TO Keeping The Fire Alive!

Rev. Kelly Fallis

authorHOUSE®

AuthorHouse™
1663 Liberty Drive
Bloomington, IN 47403
www.authorhouse.com
Phone: 1-800-839-8640

First published by AuthorHouse 1/10/2011

ISBN: 978-1-4567-1204-4 (sc)
ISBN: 978-1-4567-1205-1 (e)
ISBN: 978-1-4567-1206-8 (hc)

Library of Congress Control Number: 2010918477

Printed in the United States of America

I dedicate this book first to my Lord and Savior, Jesus Christ, to whom without His guidance and love, I could not be half the man I am. I praise you Lord Father for your kindness, your grace, your patience, your enduring faith in me, and most of all, your awesome love so abundantly shown in the precious presents you have given me in your Son and in my wife.

I also dedicate this book to my beautiful, loving wife, Amy Jo who makes it so easy to want to love her with an unquenchable desire. I praise God for the love He gives me in heaven, and for sending me an angel to love here on earth. I could not imagine life without your beauty before me, your laughter in my ear, your love within me. Thank you for honoring me with your love. Thank you for being more than just my lover and my wife, but the friend I never had until you came along.

Table of Contents

Forward 9 yrs later.......

I finished, or so I thought, writing this book in 2001 while living in Seattle and yet not only did I feel that it was unworthy to be published at the time, but that it also did not feel "complete".

Here, 9 years later and after hearing more than once from the Lord that I should publish it, (Lord, forgive me please for my hesitancy), that I finally realized what I felt was "missing" and that it is this:

<u>Love has nothing to do with sex, but sex has something to do with love.</u>

First, you will hear this again, but you might think, "what kind of double-talk it that"? My friend let me tell you, you can follow all the romantic advise in this book and I can state, your sex life *should* improve (if not then you really have some problems my friend), but if you don't *really* follow **ALL** the *advice* and really try to grasp the inner wisdom I am trying to pass along, your marriage with all its great sex will not last! Now the first question you probably have is what makes me think I'm an expert? Well, first off let me state I 'm not going to say that I'm an expert, but instead just someone who has enough experience to have the ability to pass on some wisdom and tidbits that can *help you in your marriage,* especially after 26 years of marriage and nine, yes you read right, nine children!

So, to get back to where we were; you may believe at this moment that God is talking strictly to single people when He warns of fleeing sexual immorality in I Corinthians 6:18, but I would like to point out that in verse 20 of this same chapter God says, *"For you were bought at a price; therefore glorify God in your body and in your spirit, which are God's* and, in Ephesians 5: 25 does it not say that we are to *love our wives just as Christ also loved the church and gave Himself for her*? So, therefore, how can we as husbands who are called to love our wives as Christ loved the church say we are doing so if by being romantic the only thing we are hoping for is a greater sex life? Are we not then by this spirit treating our wives as though they, too, are nothing more than harlots given to us to satisfy our physical needs? Romance my friend is not about our actions of our physical body, but of our spiritual one.

It is a spirit of romance, one of a cherishing love, that same cherishing love that Ephesians 5:29 says God has for His church, that we are to go forth and *desire* only the very best for our wives, that we may then know we can boldly go forth and ask our wives the question, "Do you know how much you are loved"? Can you today ask that question in confidence, let alone be confident in its answer? You may be surprised by their answer!

You see that was what I felt was missing from this writing; the very confidence of what I *thought* should always have been her answer. I had romanced my wife easily the first 7 years of our marriage because my walk with the Lord was strong, or so I thought; it wasn't until I went through Bible College and was ordained that the real challenges of my spiritual walk and thus my marriage were both challenged. What I am trying to say is that BOTH are inexplicably intertwined and unless you seek *that which is right first and* **foremost**, nothing you do in the physical can help the spiritual, unlike what you do with your spirit can, and does in fact, help the physical, hence; "love has nothing to do with sex, but sex has something to do with love".

When I decided to take my spiritual walk to a new level, (which, believe it or not, you are actually doing by reading this book) it was then that the enemy of my (and yours) soul brought his "A" game and has persistently attacked my marriage, that was when I found the **TRUE** meaning of romance. Yes, my friend I have to tell you that by your merely seeking to bring your love life to a new level you have decided on a spiritual level to elevate your understanding of love, and who is the author, creator and undeniably the epitome of love Himself, but Jesus Christ! Thus, you have just elevated to a new level of attacks upon your marriage. Oh great your probably thinking, thanks Guy! But really, this is in fact something to celebrate! For if the enemy is leaving you alone then you must not be doing anything to inhibit his fear. Let me encourage you to think like I do in this arena, I like to think of myself as being considered a "terrorist" in hell, I pray and fight for my picture to be placed on posters within the enemy's post offices down in hell that read, **"WANTED DEAD"**, BEFORE HE DESTROYS ANYMORE OF OUR PLANS TO THWART THE PLANS OF GOD! I challenge you to not read this book with the mindset of improving your sex life, but instead, improving your *love* life.

When you fully understand the difference you have not only truly matured, but have elevated your marriage to a new and exciting level.

I don't want anyone to think that by picking up this book it is somehow going to transform their marriage unless they understand that the only book that is really important to read and understand is the one written by the Lord Himself, His Holy Bible. The GREATEST Romantic Love Story Ever Written!

That is the TRUE self-help book that can help in every area of your life. This book here I hope will only help to awaken what is already in you or, help guide you into a new way of thinking and approaching your bride. The beautiful, precious present He has given you in the gift of His daughter, your wife.

There is only one who never fails and that is the Father! We as human beings will only succeed if we are willing to admit our mistakes and failures and realize that we don't know it all. If you want to know what your spouse is thinking you MUST communicate and ask questions, and then not only be ready to hear the answer, but be able to accept it as how she feels, *regardless* of whether it agrees with what you think or not!

You can choose to love someone despite their faults and differences in opinions just like she must choose to love you despite YOUR faults and opinions. And believe me, YOU do have faults! The only perfect one who ever roamed this earth was named Jesus Christ!

The Father is the ONLY answer and unless you seek Him diligently in every aspect of your life, especially in your marriage and love life, no self-help book will ever be able to deliver you to that place of peace and rest.

Chapter One

True Love

Since the dawn of time man has asked the ever eluding question; what is the true meaning of love"?

No matter where one may look, all that is seen are differing views and meanings of this mysterious question handed down through the generations.

Sadly the answer to this ever-eluding question has mistakenly been the beginning of many relationships and the start of many marriages. The reason I say sadly is because once the happily married newlyweds realized that what they thought it was, which like us all, was anything but the true meaning, they inevitably call it quits, only to move on to the next relationship with the same question at hand. Nowhere is this scenario played out more than within Christ's own earthly body, the Church! There are more divorces today within the Body of Christ than there are reported within the secular world. The reasons are numerous, some even downright ignorant.

How many Pastor's do we hear talk about how God wants us to be happy which, without the proper clarification and teaching of exactly what that means, is translated into, "well my husband (or wife) just doesn't satisfy me anymore, or just doesn't understand me; surely God wants me to be happy so He won't mind if I get a divorce". It's amazing how we can twist God's words so that they suit what it is we need and not Him! Did you ever stop to think that perhaps God is not so much concerned with your happiness as He is with your soul? Do you think that perhaps that was what Paul was referring to when he was left in prison?

What is just as sad, especially within the body of Christ, is the ignorance to the fact that this very question has been answered since the dawn of time; we've just never paid any attention to it. It was more because of our own disbelief or confusion about the very author himself, rather than the true answer that has lain before us.

Or, in the case of The Church, its the lack of desire to truly seek out the answers to the questions we have, in part, because we know deep down inside the answer we find will probably not be the one we want in the flesh.

You see we have all heard, and on one occasion or another since our youth, either spoken of, or seen, some kind of a scenario play out that told us of this ever-elusive "GOD". But yet we could not seem to lay our finger on exactly who, or what, this entity was. So if we didn't really have a true sense of who He might be, we weren't about to seek out an answer from what we didn't understand, let alone believe that He had the answer to what has been one of man's most difficult questions:

What is true love?

And yet the answer has lain before us, like a treasure waiting to be discovered if but one would believe in treasure maps. Yes, God has given us that treasure map but we have either read it and only wanted to believe those sections that would pertain to our life, or, pass it off as some far fetched story of some great imaginations handed down through the years. This great treasure map ladies and gentlemen is called the Bible.

We read all about great love relationships in the Old Testament like Abraham and Sarah or Jacob and Rachel and yet not one of these relationships faired any better than those today. There was adultery, lust and just as much deceitfulness as any marriage today. Why?

Simply because they, just like us have failed to look to the very creator, who is the very essence, the presence, the magnifier, the supplier, the giver, the river, the emancipation of, the declaration of and the final authority of love Himself, the Lord Jesus Christ, for their answer.

God, our Father, our creator desires us to have the very thing He created us for, an intimate relationship. He knew that sin had not only separated man from Himself but that there was a lack of any true love within the human race. Let's face it; animal sacrifices but were a temporal bridge at best. Man was simply inept to grasp a covenant covered by the blood of an animal. So our Father decided to send His one and only Son to not only be a bridge between us, to be the ultimate and final sacrifice, to be a new covenant, but that prayerfully, lovingly, by sacrificing His only and only begotten Son, that perhaps finally man would see just how much the Father truly loved us. Perhaps man would finally understand what true love really was supposed to look like! Perhaps He could teach us the true meaning of love, by being love itself.

He knew that if He could somehow get us to understand the true love that He had for us, by being the perfect example of love that perhaps we would begin to share His love for us with one another.

So God gave us His one and only Son, Jesus Christ.

This is how God expressed His love for us!

We expressed ours how? By crucifying Him!

Yes, that's our love!

So our Creator, the ever patient, ever slow to anger Father that He is, through the power of The Holy Spirit, instilled upon man the answer and had him write it down, the ultimate description of true love. Paul, in his letter to the Corinthians, inscribed to us the perfect description of what the perfect love truly looks and acts like. Never before, nor since, has there been a greater description of what true love really is then those eloquent words written in 1 Corinthians 13:

(1) Though I speak with the tongues of men and of angels but have not love, I have become but a resounding gong or a clanging symbol. (2) And though I have the gift of prophecy to understand all mysteries and all knowledge; and though I have all faith, so that I could remove mountains, but have not love, I am nothing. (3) And though I bestow all my goods to feed the poor, and though I present my body to be burned, but have not love, it profits me nothing. (4) Love suffers long and is kind. Love does not envy, love does not parade itself, is not puffed up;(5) does not behave rudely, does not seek it's own, is not provoked, thinks no evil;(6) does not rejoice in inequity, but rejoices in the truth;(7) bears all thing, believes all things, hopes all things, endures all things. (8) Love never fails. But whether there are prophecies, they will fail, whether there are tongues they shall cease, whether there is knowledge, it will vanish away. (9) For we know in part and we prophesy in part. (10) But when that which is perfect has come, than that which is in part will be done away. (11) When I was a child, I spoke as a child, I thought as a child, I understood as a child, But when I

became a man I put away childish things. (12) For now we see in a mirror dimly, but then face to face. For now I know in part, but then I shall be known just as I also am known. (13) And now abide faith, hope, love, these three; BUT THE GREATEST OF THESE IS LOVE. (Capitalization is mine)

Now guys you will notice in verse 8 it does not say that love may fail, or that it can fail, or even that it is going to fail, NO, God's word says that LOVE NEVER FAILS!!!

He says it <u>bears all</u>, <u>believes all</u>, <u>hopes all</u>, and <u>endures all</u>. Not, well my lying eyes saw her talking with that guy at the store and I wouldn't doubt she probably has something going on. No, when God says to believe all, He doesn't mean believe all the bad you can about your spouse, but instead to give her the benefit of the doubt.

Not to listen to the little doubts that Satan likes to plant in our minds, but instead to believe in the covenant that you both swore your love on and too. To endure all those nagging questions that will be thrown at you and instead look to Him for strength in your time of weakness. To bear all the temptations that you two will be put through in Satan's attempt to destroy that, which God has brought together. Its so funny to hear how many men and women make the statement that when they get married they will settle down, as though somehow a written document or the mere fact that they made a declaration of, "I do", will somehow make them invulnerable to the temptations of the flesh. As though Satan is going to go," "Oh well they're married now I guess I have to leave them alone!" Marriage my friends is the foundation of the Kingdom of God, *"Therefore a man shall leave his father and mother and be joined to his wife, and they shall become one flesh" (Gen 2:24)* and no one understands this better than Satan! He will do EVERYTHING HE CAN to destroy it!. *1 Peter 5:8* says; *"Be sober, be vigilant; because your adversary the devil walks about like a roaring lion, seeking whom he may devour"*.

If we are to endure it must be as one together, not as separate entities looking out for our own self-interests.

There are more proverbial scriptures based on adultery than any other subject. Do you suppose God is trying to tell us something?

Let's review some of **His wisdom**:

"To deliver you from the immoral women, from the seductress who flatters with her words, who forsakes the covenant of her God. For her house leads down to death, and her paths to the dead. None who go to her return, nor do they regain the paths of life. Prov 2:16-19

Explanation For The 21st Centurion:

Look guys, my wisdom will keep you from the tramp who messes with your mind by making you think your The Rock. Sleep with her and your life is over, as you know it. You WILL NOT be able to "take-it-back" and the pain you will inflict will last forever. And if you happen to be married to one of those roller-derby babes, you just may not wake up the next morning either!

His wisdom:

"My son, pay attention to my wisdom; Lend your ear to my understanding, that you may preserved discretion, and your lips may keep knowledge, For the immoral woman drip honey and her mouth is smoother than oil; But in the end she is bitter as wormwood. Sharp as a two-edged sword. Her feet go down to death. Her steps lay hold of hell. Lest you ponder her path of life, Her ways are unstable; you do not know them. Therefore hear me

now, my children, and do not depart from the words of my mouth. Remove your way far from her, and do not go near the door of her house, lest you give your honor to others and your years to the cruel one; lest aliens be filled with your wealth and your labors go to the house of a foreigner; and you mourn at last. When your flesh and your body are consumed, and say: How I have hated instruction, and my heart despised correction! I have not obeyed the voice of teachers, nor inclined my ear to those who instructed me! Prov 5:1-13

Explanation For The 21st Centurion:

You should have listened to me! Stay away!

His wisdom:

"To keep you from the evil woman, from the flattering tongue of a seductress. Do not lust after her beauty in your heart, nor let her allure you with her eyelids. For by means of a harlot A man is reduced to a crust of bread' and an adulteress will prey upon his precious life. Can a man take fire to his bosom and not be burned? Can one walk on coals and his feet not be seared? So is he who goes into his neighbor's wife: Whoever touches her will not be innocent. Prov 6:24-29

Explanation For The 21st Centurion:

If she winks at you RUN! The beautiful babe next door, forget about it!

His wisdom:

"Whoever commits adultery with a woman lacks understanding; He who does so destroys his own soul. Wounds and dishonor he will get; and his reproach will not be wiped away, for jealousy is a husband's fury; therefore

he will not spare in the day of vengeance. He will accept no recompense, nor will he be appeased though you give many gifts". Prov 6:32-35

Explanation For The 21st Centurion:

If you think he's going to "forget about it", your crazier than you think!

His wisdom:

"For at the window of my house I looked through my lattice, and saw among the simple, I perceived among the youths, A young man devoid of understanding, Passing along the street near her corner; And he took the path to her house, In the twilight, in the evening, In the black and dark of night. And there a woman met him, with the attire of a harlot, and a crafty heart. She was loud and rebellious; Her feet would not stay at home. At times she was outside, at times in the open square, Lurking at every corner, So she caught him and kissed him; With an impudent face she said to him: "I have peace offerings with me; Today I have paid my vows. So I came out to meet you, Diligently to seek your face, and I have found you. I have spread my bed with tapestry, colored coverings of Egyptian linen. I have perfumed my bed with myrrh, aloes and cinnamon. Come, let us take our fill until morning; Let us delight ourselves with love. For my husband is not at home; He has gone on a long journey; He has taken a bag of money with him and will come home on the appointed day." With her enticing speech she caused him to yield, with her flattering lips she seduced him. Immediately he went after her as an ox goes to slaughter, Or as a fool to the correction of the stocks, till an arrow struck his liver. As a bird hastens to the snare, He did not know it would cost him his life". Prov 7:6-23

Explanation For The 21st Centurion:

It's amazing how many people think they can get away with an affair! If the devil allowed you to get away with it his LIE would not be working. He MUST have the affair found out in order for the lie to work, thus breaking up the marriage.

Just because she says he isn't around doesn't mean it's true! Adultery is not worth your life, his life, your wife's or your children! That's why God says FLEE!

FLEE from the woman who flatters you, after all, face it bud, you aren't THAT HOT!

So you think you can handle a little flattery and batting of the eyes! Listen to what The Father says:

Now therefore, Listen to me, my children; Pay attention to the words of my mouth; Do not let your heart turn aside to her ways. Do not stray into her paths: For she has cast down many wounded. ***And all who were slain by her were strong men.*** *(Boldness mine) Her house is the way to hell, Descending to the chambers of death. Prov 7:24-27*

There are other words of wisdom that deal with adultery that you can find in the following Proverbs: 9:13-18, 11:6, 17:19, 22:14 23:27-28, 28:10, and 28:18

Bottom-line guys is adultery is spiritually, morally, and ethically wrong and there has never been ANY GOOD that has ever derived from it.

Remember: Ignorance Is: The lack of knowledge in a particular area or subject.

Stupidity is: Having that knowledge and refusing to use it.

It's OKAY to be ignorant at first, this is what education or knowledge is used for, to erase it. It is NOT OK to be willfully stupid!

To love the wife that God has given you becomes even easier when we seek His ways in doing so:

In Ephesians 5:25 we read:

Husbands love your wives **as** Christ so loved the church. (*italics mine*)

Guys, this little two-letter word, **AS,** is the most defining statement in the Bible in how God expects you to love your wife. How did Christ love the church? He DIED for it. Now I know the first place your going to go is, "well I'd die for my wife". Sorry Guys, it's not that kind of death. Of course if something came against your wife we wouldn't think twice about laying down our life to protect her (at least I hope so guys or we need to talk ☺), no, the death I'm talking about is can you die to yourself on a daily basis? Can you wake up in the morning and instead of thinking about how you are doing; think about her and what can you do on this particular day to make her day brighter.

I know that this can be a tall order and one that seems impossible to fill at times, but the great news is that after God told us how we are supposed to love, He also gave us the biblical roadmap leading us to the strength we will need;

In Ephesians 6:10-17 He says;

Finally, my brethren, be strong in the Lord and in the power of His might.

*Put on the whole armor of God, that you may be **able to stand** against the wiles of the devil.*

For we do not wrestle against flesh and blood, but against principalities, against powers, against the rulers of the darkness of this age, against spiritual hosts of wickedness in the heavenly places.

*Therefore **take up** the **whole armor** of God, that you may be able to **withstand** in the evil day, and having done all, to **stand**.*

***STAND**, therefore, having girded your waist with truth, having put on the breastplate of righteousness.*

And having shod your feet with the preparation of the gospel of peace;

*Above all, **taking the shield of faith** with which you will be able to quench all the fiery darts of the wicked one.*

*And **take the helmet of salvation**, and the **sword of the Spirit**, which is the word of God.*

Though this is taken from the New King James Version, as all scriptural references, unless otherwise noted, the **bolded Italics** is mine to point out the key things God expects you to do.

So you see God has not only answered, but also in fact been THE answer to the question that has eluded us all along, what is true love? We just failed to both look hard enough for the answer, or showed enough faith in the author Himself.

So now that you have the answer your next question may be,

"How are we, as men, supposed to fill this role?"

That is a question I hope this book will give you some answers to. I won't claim it is the best written on the subject or answers it completely. Instead I hope it is just a tool that you can use as a reference to help you in how to make your bride feel like the Queen that the Lord intended her to be in your life. If you begin to apply the principles set down in this book, and take the knowledge given by our precious Lord in His word, the Bible, your spirit, your love and your marriage will change, period.

Base your love, your marriage and your romance on the Rock. You can never go wrong by doing so!

Chapter Two

The Four Precious Presents

In 1995, just before my wife and I left Rochester New York to what has amounted to a journey toward a greater relationship with our Lord, I was approached by our then, Sr. Youth Pastor who I had the honor to work with for a few years.

He had always spoken publicly to the young men of the youth group that if they ever wanted to know how to properly romance a lady, they should come to me, for as he put it, Kelly doesn't DO Romance, Kelly IS Romance.

He said to me that I should write a book about Romance, God's way. I took it as a compliment, but at the same time blew it off as just that. Surely he couldn't have meant it, let alone thought I was worthy enough to do so. Just before we left his sentiment was backed up by another one of the youth leaders. Again, I felt it was just a departing compliment. Surely he didn't actually feel I was worthy to do such a task.

I knew I didn't feel worthy enough.

September 1998. I was sitting 8 rows back; about the 8th seat in listening to Kenneth Copeland speak on faith and prosperity when I heard HIS voice. It was as audible as it is when your friend or spouse talks to you; only I knew it was only I He was speaking to. "Kelly", yes Lord was my reply (after all what else you going to say to God, go away!). "Do you remember that poem you wrote a few years back about the precious present"? Yes Father! " Well I want you to write a book, only I want you to tell them about my four precious presents".

Four Father.

"Yes son, you spoke about my second when you spoke about life, but I want you to tell about all four".

"Now Kelly, this is how I want you to start the book"...The Lord then went on to explain His Four Precious Presents:

Precious Present One

The Earth

In the beginning God created the heavens and the earth: Gen 1:1

Then God said, "Let the waters under the heavens be gathered together into one place, and let the dry land appear: and it was so; And God called the dry land Earth, and the gathering of the together of the waters He called the Seas. And God saw that it was good. Gen 2:9

Imagine yourself in a world where everything is absolutely perfect. Lush forests thick with towering trees, water cascading down mountains of crimson reds and desert browns into crystal clear ponds whose shades of blues are brighter than the skies above.

Skies that seem to go on forever washed in shades of turquoise and baby blues, the sun seeming to radiate from an orange orbit larger than the universe. Oceans and seas that abound with an abundance of life while on the land animals frolicked in the valley as though they were born of the same mother. Antelope running along side the bear, lions licking baby lambs to comfort them, birds with wingspans that seemed to stretch from one mountain peak to the next, charging toward one another and swiftly veering off in a game of aerial tag. Not a one with any fear of an enemy. Yes, a world where EVERYTHING was perfect. A place where the word violence, let alone its very presence, did not exist.

There was NO pollution of any kind! No trash pollution, no water pollution, no air pollution. There were no sicknesses or diseases. No E-Coli, Diphtheria, STD's, Polio, Cancer, Leukemia, MDS, Bi-Polar or any other mind or body dysfunctions.

There were no storms or violent thrashings of nature unleashing its fury on the earth. The plants and trees received their nourishment from rich soil that was watered by a fine mist that rose from the ground. It was a place of perfect harmony. Where the sounds would lull you to sleep and the air was as crisp as a white linen sheet pressed and starched from the laundry.

There was NOTHING out of place, and everything was in its perfect place.

This was Earth as God had created it.

Hard to imagine huh?

It was a world that really even in our finest dreams we could not yet begin to comprehend the beauty of it.

But God being the Supreme Being that He is, the creator and Sustainer of all that lives and the very essence of love did not stop there, no there was a purpose for this perfect place under heaven. He was not done creating yet, no the creator Himself was just getting started:

Precious Present Two

Life

And the Lord God formed man of the dust of the ground, and breathed into his nostrils the breath of life; and man became a living soul. Gen 2:7

Can you imagine as God breathed forth life into Adam and Adam opened his eyes for the first time, picture him laying there on the ground and looking up and seeing his Father, the One, the only true living God looking down on Him, a look of total satisfaction and happiness radiating forth from His smile. (Though this may not of happened just humor me)

Imagine Adam's thoughts when God said here let me help you up, come my son I have a present I wish to give you and then bringing him forth into the Garden of Eden.

The Garden of Eden, it's meaning according to the American Dictionary of The English Language Noah Webster 1828, is *pleasure, delight*. I can just see Adam twirling around, trying desperately to take in all the sights and sounds before him and exclaiming, "WOW! This is magnificent Father!"

The perfect home. Not only did Adam have the perfect home, but also he had GOD as his best friend! Imagine having such a close relationship with the Lord that He asks YOU to name all the beasts of the earth for HIM!!! Can you imagine how special Adam must have felt?

My Lord you want me to what…name the animals for you….but what if I come up with something stupid….and I could imagine God's gentle voice saying, Nothing my Son that I have created can be stupid.

Ok Father, that one looks kind of funny, lets call it an Aardvark.

Aardvark…sounds good to me Son…continue. *And Adam gave names to all cattle, and the fowl of the air, and to every beast of the field; Gen 2:20*

Adam got to do everything with and for God, after all in God's eyes Adam was perfect;

And God said, Let us make man in our image, Gen 1:26.

Imagine what is must have felt like to Adam to be able to walk hand in hand with God through this perfect place. Yes, it was perfect in Adam's eye but NOT in God's. He knew there was something missing..

And the Lord God said, It is not good that the man should be alone; I will make him an help meet for him. Gen 2:18

Precious Present 3

A Wife

So God gave Adam His 3rd most precious present: a Wife.

And the Lord God caused a deep sleep to fall upon Adam and he slept: and he took one of his ribs, and closed up the flesh instead thereof:

And the rib, which the Lord God had taken from man, made he a woman, and brought her unto the man.

And Adam said, This is now bone of my bones, and flesh of my flesh: she shall be called Woman, because she was taken out of Man.

Therefore shall a man leave his father and his mother, and shall cleave unto his wife: and they shall be ONE flesh. Gen 2:22-25

Now guys you may think Sophia Loren or Raquel Welch are beautiful, too old school for some of you young ones, ok, how about Jennifer Aston, or Angelina Jolie, these ladies gentlemen couldn't even compare to Eve! Eve HAD to be perfect!

Perfect in body and every other sense to Adam.

After all do you think God would have given anything LESS to His friend?

But when Adam first viewed Eve he didn't start panting all over himself with wanton lust. No he LOVED her with a pure heart. Keep in mind that sin had not entered into the world. Adam viewed Eve, just as God did, he was created in God's image, therefore his thoughts toward Eve were as pure as humanly possible, again, keep in mind that sin had not yet entered into the Garden. Lust, guys, is sin, this is why Adam could not have looked at Eve, who was standing there IN THE FLESH in such a manner.

But then **man's** first sin occurred. Now I know most of you are thinking, yeah, Eve ate the apple from the tree of Knowledge of Good and Evil. Wrong. It was the man who first sinned because of his failure to take his rightful dominion OVER that serpent and PROTECT his wife;

And God said, let us make man in our image, after our likeness: and let them have dominion over the fish of the sea, and over the fowl of the air, and over the cattle, and over ALL the earth, and over every creeping thing that creepeth upon the earth. Gen 1:26

If Adam had taken dominion OVER that serpent, the dominion God had given him, and cast it out of the garden, and had told his wife, you shall not eat of that tree, sin would never had entered the earth. But because Adam FAILED in his Godly role as the head of the household, because He FAILED his wife whom God had given him, because HE did not look to God for his strength in his time of weakness, HE failed his wife, his wife did not fail him.

Since that time of sin, man immediately began to blame the woman for his own weaknesses;

And the man said, The woman whom thou gavest to be with me, SHE gave me of the tree and I did eat. Gen 4:12

God went on to tell Adam of his failure to take his proper dominion;

And unto Adam he said, Because thou hast hearkened unto the voice of thy wife, and hast eaten of the tree, of which I commanded thee, saying, Thou shalt not eat of it: cursed is the ground for thy sake: in sorrow shalt thou eat of it all the days of thy life. Gen 4:17

Since then, instead of viewing our wife as the precious present God had intended her to be, we've used, abused, beaten, raped; we've corrupted and hated and yes, even killed.

Like a spoiled angry child who wasn't satisfied with the gift our parents labored so hard, and saved so long to give us trying to give us their very best, we have simply tossed it aside.

Now one would think that most people would just throw their hands up in the air in disgust and say," FINE, you don't want what I have to offer, then fend for yourself"! I QUIT!

Yes, most of us humans would simply have given up, but not our Father, the Creator and Sustainer of all that lives. Not our one and only true living God!

Instead He decided He would give us one more present….His most precious present of all….

Precious Present Four

His SON

JESUS The CHRIST

His one and only begotten son, Jesus.

He brought him here to become the purest and truest sacrifice in order that we could live an eternal life with Him who created us. He brought Him here to teach us how to live, to show us how to love. To love with a pure heart. A love purer than the finest gold, softer than the finest silk, sweeter than the sweetest honey. He brought Him here to be the ultimate of sacrifices, to be the last, to be the everlasting symbol of a newer, better covenant.

And what did we do with this, this most precious present of all…..

WE KILLED HIM!

Yes, it was to fulfill scripture so that by His sacrifice the law may be fulfilled and that a new covenant between the Creator and the created be once again firmly established in the heavens, with us once again tasting the Father's sweet love for us.

For if that first covenant had been faultless, then no place would have been sought for a second. Because finding fault with them, He says: "Behold the days are coming, says the Lord, when I will make a new covenant with the house of Judah- "not according to the covenant I made with their fathers in the day when I took them by the hand to lead them out of the land of Egypt; because they did not continue in My covenant, and I disregarded them say the Lord. For this is the covenant that I will make with the house of Israel after those days, says the Lord: I will put My laws in their mind and write them on their hearts; and I will be their God, and they shall be my people. Heb 8:7-11

For our God to raise His only begotten Son from the dead to be seated at His right hand, to be our intercessor, to once again be our example of what true love does for those it loves; to stand in the gap and speak only blessings over that which he loves, took a love far greater than any *Webster's* Dictionary could define.

For it was fitting for Him, for whom are all things and by whom are all things, in bringing many sons to glory, to make the captain of their salvation perfect through sufferings. For both He who sanctifies and those who are being sanctified are all of one, for which reason He is not ashamed to call them brethren, saying:

I will declare Your name to My brethren;

In the midst of the assembly I will sing praise to you." Heb 2:10-12

Yes, to once again teach us how to give, to show us how to live, to show us once again, the TRUE meaning of LOVE.

By now you are probably saying, okay, so what does all this have to do with romance, what could the four precious presents possibly have to do with romancing your wife?

Well, first you have to have established in your heart how special your wife truly is in the eyes of the Lord. How much He not only loves her, but how much He loved you when He created her just for you.

You have to understand that it isn't just any woman standing before you, but she is the daughter of Christ, created by Him, for you, to love as He loves. To honor as He honors; To cherish the way He cherishes; To respect as He respects.

We have to eliminate from our minds the world's view of the very definition of the word love. If you were to go by the world's definition or view you have to talk about a feeling; *Monday,* "oh, I am so in love with you sweetheart, I don't know what I would do without you".

Then on Tuesday we get into an argument with her only to say, "Dear I've decided I don't love you anymore, you don't understand me, I've simply fallen out of love with you and I want a divorce"!

"O wow! I just LOVE that car!"

"Ah man, I just LOVE this pizza!"

"Gosh, I just love the feeling of this blouse next to my skin".

This people, is the world's view and definition of love. It is but a *feeling* that can come and go with the rising of the tide or the setting of the sun.

Sadly, it is this definition that many a marriage has been begun on, thus also the failure because *"emotions or feelings"* change!

But you see Jesus' love is not like some pit you fall in and out of. It is THE way the heart, spirit and mind all come together in perfect harmony. A place where you know this is what is meant by the phrase" Heaven on Earth".

No such love you say…. your only kidding yourself. No one can have this kind of love for one another you say.

Well in order to understand how the Lord wants us to view our marriage, and our wife, we have to look to Ephesians 5 17 – 29:

Wherefore be ye not unwise, but understanding what the will of the Lord is. And be not drunk with wine, wherein is excess; but be filled with the Spirit; Heb 5:17-18

Speaking to yourselves in psalms and hymns and spiritual songs, singing and making melody in your hearts to the Lord. Giving thanks always for all things unto God and the Father in the name of our Lord Jesus Christ; Submitting yourselves one to another in the fear of God. Wives, submit yourselves unto your own husbands, as unto the Lord. For the husband is the head of the wife, even as Christ is the head of the church: and he is the savoir of the body. Therefore as the church is subject unto Christ, so let the wives be to their own husbands in everything. Heb 5:19-24

Did you know that by speaking in love to your wife it actually brings joy to the Lord? It pleases Him when He see the two people who He had planned from birth, to bring together in His perfect will, speaking and acting in love toward one another.

There are those who say show me a couple that don't bicker and fight and I'll show you a couple not in love. I disagree and so does God.

It is not in His will for His children to bicker and fight with one another. It is however ok to have disagreements or differences of opinions, and yes, there is a difference. Bickering and fighting does not get a relationship ANYWHERE; having a dialog does. When you start to bicker and fight you lose the ability to have a conversation where both parties feel they are being heard, instead of that, all that is coming out are hurt feelings and words that damage the relationship, not build it up. Again, His word says that we are to edify each other. Bickering and fighting do not accomplish this! Period!

In the above passage, it says to submit yourselves to one another; the word submit means to yield your will. It doesn't say let the strongest one get their way.

It also says; "For the husband is the head of the wife". However this **DOESN'T say that he is the BOSS**. A head is supposed to act as a stabilizer, someone who is responsible for the family, not a person who is irresponsible and uncaring, who only want things his way on his time and his terms.

Sadly there are so many Christian men today who use that scripture as an excuse to abuse and boss their wives around. They are so quick to skip over verse 21 which, I will repeat, says, "submitting to one another in the fear of God" and instead they take verse 22 vastly out of context, and then have the audacity to wonder why the divorce rate is just as high if not higher in the church than it is in society as a whole.

It is because we hide behind our "holiness" as we use and abuse that which God created for us all the while taking His word and twisting it so that it suits our needs!

We must whenever using or quoting scripture to never take it out of context. For instance many men as I have said take verse 22 as a stand-alone verse that means I AM BOSS but yet if you continue reading and get to verse 25,

'*Husbands, love your wives, even as Christ also loved the church and gave himself for it*', *Eph 5:25.*

How can you after reading this, if you apply any logic, say you are loving love your wife as Christ loves the church if you are abusing the authority God has given you?

Gentlemen verse 25 defines the kind of love God COMMANDS us to give to our wives and it is this single passage that is the true foundation and subject of this book. That two letter word, **AS,** is one of the most defining words of what God wants a man to define his own love after.

AS Christ also LOVED the church.

A love this deep does not bicker and fight, it doesn't try to define what the relationship should be. It doesn't say we will do things my way or no way at all. Instead it listens and learns. It knows when to be strong, when one should compromise or even admit its wrong. To say hey Hon, lets do it your way when her way is best. Are you so arrogant as to think God only speaks to you?

It is a love that is willing to give even its very life away to save that of another.

To love your wife as Christ also love the church is to give your wife a love that is far beyond the world's definition of love. For as it states in Eph 6:28-33:

So ought men to love their wives as their own bodies. He that loveth his wife loveth himself.

For no man ever yet hated his own flesh; but nourisheth and cherisheth it, even as the Lord the church. For we are members of his body, of his flesh, and of his bones. For this cause shall a man leave his father and mother, and shall be joined unto his wife, and the two shall be one flesh. This is a great mystery: but I speak concerning Christ and the church. Nevertheless, let every one of you in particular so love his wife even as himself; and the wife see that she reverence her husband.

Now guys this is NOT a one-way street for as Eph 6:33 above points out to the wives,

"and the wife see that she reverence her husband".

God expects us to love and reverence one another.

He expects us to edify one another, to lift each other up and to always look out for one another no matter HOW HARD times may get. In fact to say during those most hardest of times, "it's ok Hon what we may go through, as long as I have you in the end, I know that together, with Him, we can overcome all!"

"This I say, therefore, and testify in the Lord, that you should no longer walk as the rest of the Gentiles walk, in the futility of their mind, having their understanding darkened, being alienated from the life of God, because of the ignorance that is in them, because of the blindness of their heart; who, being past feeling, have given themselves over to lewdness, to work all uncleanness with greediness.

But you have not so learned Christ, if indeed you have heard Him and have been taught y Him, as the truth is in Jesus: that you put off, concerning your former conduct, the old man which grows corrupt according to the deceitful lusts, and be renewed in the spirit of your mind, and that you put on the new man which was created according to God, in true righteousness and holiness.

Therefore, putting away lying, "Let each of you speak truth with his neighbor, for we are members of one another. Eph 4:17-25

Let no corrupt word proceed out of your mouth, but what is good for necessary edification, that it may impart grace to the hearers. Eph 4:29

And be kind to one another, tenderhearted, forgiving one another, even as God in Christ forgave you. Eph 4:32

So you see it is through His most precious present of all, His son Jesus Christ that we can look to define what the REAL meaning of love is all about.

Chapter Three
Being Romantic

There is a big difference between being a romantic and doing romance. Anyone can do romance.

You make reservations at a nice restaurant, eat dinner by candlelight, go dancing afterwards, and waa-laaa you have romance.

However to have romance flow through you like blood flows through your veins takes more than just a candle light dinner. The very essence of the spirit of romance is more that just a fleeting moment in time, it is the ever-present presence of His love flowing through you. For you to know and feel blessed to the very fiber of your soul that you, yes you, have been honored by the very presence of such a precious present that he has given you in your wife, your lady, your love. The very presence of my wife entering the same room I am in makes me want to sweep her off her feet, to cherish her and to make sure she knows, without the slightest doubt in her heart, how much she is truly loved.

Now I know that you are probably thinking, "I bet you don't feel that way when you're having a disagreement", but actually you couldn't be further from the truth.

You see when God said in Gen 2:18,

I will make him a helpmate,

He wasn't talking about someone who will clean his house or cook his meals, but someone who would be able to show him not only his strengths, but his weaknesses as well.

You see Guys woman was taken from man's SIDE, not his back, God created the woman to come along SIDE her man.

I praise God for the wisdom he has given my wife, and yes I am grateful for the correction she gives me.

She is the mirror to my soul.

A great and godly man I loved, admired and respected, the late Dr Edwin Cole, founder and President of the world renowned Christian Men's Network once said, "Great is the man who can look beyond himself and instead look into the heart of his woman, for it is there that God has planted his greatest vision of what He, not you, knows you can be".

That's right!

You see God knew from the start who He, not you, wanted you to marry. He also knew that since he created her with the power to look to the heart, where men tend to count on their intellect, that if He could get us to see and become even half the man of that vision, we'd be great men of God. Worthy not only of his precious present, but would then also be able to be the soldiers he needs us to be to carry on His love.

I know this and that is why even in times where we forget to look to

Him and our personalities get ahead of His principalities, my heart still jumps every time she walks into the room.

I WANT to become the man that she envisions.

Now some will say, "why can't she just love you just the way you are"? That's a part of the absolute beauty and what makes her the precious present she is; she DOES love me unconditionally. She ACTUALLY loves the man she married and if I never reached the potential of the vision that God has revealed to her in her heart, she would still love me with the greatness that she does until the day I die and beyond. This is one of the things that makes it even easier to have the romance and passion that I have for her. This is what makes it so much more desirable to want to become the man she envisions.

Men understand one thing; God has a greater plan for you than where you are at right now. Far greater, greater than any dream or vision you could ever have. His love is far greater than any love you have ever felt and it all starts with the precious presents He has given you in His son Jesus Christ, and His daughter, the wife he has presented to you.

When you feel like you are going through tough times remember His word says to have faith.

What is faith? In Hebrews 11:1 it says,

Now faith is the substance of things hoped for, the evidence of things not seen.

So to have a love that can get you through any argument is to look at your wife with the same eyes that God had when He created her just for you. That instead of always wanting your way, allow yourself the ability to step out of yourself, to step outside the box as they say, and look to her to see yourself in a different light. Don't allow Satan to put blinders on you so that you miss the opportunity to be a better man. Don't allow pride, which is a tool Satan uses to rob you of everything good around you, to stop yourself from receiving the love and the wisdom He has given your wife for you. If you look at Proverbs 12:1 you will see that God says, *"Whoever loves instruction loves knowledge, but he who hates correction is stupid".*

That's right, that's God's word, not mine; He says to not except correction is stupid.

Don't be stupid, foolish, ignorant or pig headed, if God gives your wife insight into a situation your involved in, be smart enough to listen to her. Your not the only one God speaks to.

Now there are some of you who may say, "yea, well I've seen what my wife wants me to become, or hey I've seen what my friend has become trying to change for his wife; I don't want no part with it". I couldn't agree with you more, but based on one very important point: You see in my first marriage, one where neither of us knew the Lord, let alone had any kind of a relationship with Him, I was CONSTANTLY trying to change to be what my ex-wife wanted me to be, but was anything but what my Lord wanted me to be. I changed so many times that in the end, I was so far lost inside neither of us knew who I was, let alone what she wanted me to be to begin with. The difference between my first marriage and my second is that my first wife's view was based off of her worldly views, most of which were made up from what she had seen in her own household, as well as the environment around her, but my second wife's view is based off her spiritual understanding of who she is, as well as who I am, in the Lord.

My first marriage is like the Lord's saying in Matthew 7:27;

"and the rain descended, the floods came, and the winds blew and beat on that house; and it fell. And great was its fall.

My second marriage however is totally built on the scripture preceding this; Matthew 7:25;

"And the rain descended, the floods came, and the winds blew and beat on that house; and it did not fall, for it was founded on the rock.

You have choices in your marriage, you can choose to follow the course that is laid down by the world before you, with it's ever changing views and philosophies, or you can say, I choose to follow the Rock.

If you say, "Kelly I WANT MY MARRIAGE TO SUCCEED AND I'M WILLING TO DO WHATEVER IT TAKES TO MAKE THAT HAPPEN, then the first thing you must do is you must be willing to turn your life and your marriage over to God. It is only He that can give *both* of you a strength to brave the onslaught of the world's waves of mediocrity, complacency, degradation and finally, destruction that Satan is waiting to wreck on the partnership that God has brought together.

If you are *both* grounded in Him, if your marriage is built on the ROCK, when you look to her heart, you will only see the radiance of the love that He has for you both.

Folks this is not a one person only kind of way, it must be a together we can conquer the world kind of thing. But men, let there be no doubt, it starts with you! You are whom God has called to take the lead. Do you dare?

I challenge you:

Grab hold of His ways, His love, and apply it to your marriage; it will take you to new heights.

Chapter Four

Respect

One of the quickest ways to lose the romance out of a relationship is for your wife or your lady to lose respect for you. I don't care what type of home life – work relationship you may have, be it she's a career woman or a stay at home Mom, your lady <u>does</u> look up to you. And if you are out in the world making decisions or acting "stupid" without considering the consequences it will have on your family or your relationship with her, don't look for the candle to burn too long.

There was once this couple I knew who seemed to everyone around them to be this totally together, "perfect" family. However behind closed doors what you had was a relationship that was going south. One of the problems was the gentleman was laid off from work, and with this layoff came severance pay; so this gentleman using the excuse, "God will provide" and "Honey, we have to have faith", sat on his laurels. Now when I say excuse, I don't mean that we should NOT have faith, for even the Lord's word says in Hebrews 10:23, *"Let us hold fast the profession of our faith without wavering"*,

as well as in Ephesians 3:20;
Now to him who is able to do exceedingly abundantly above all that we ask

or think, *according to the power that works within us;* however neither of these scriptures said, sit on thy butt my son for I shall have the next employer knock on your door". No, God expects us to put one foot in front of the other just like our wife's and family do, to go out and knock on some doors. As His word says in Matthew 7:7-9,

"Ask and it will be given you; seek and you shall find, knock and the door will be opened, For everyone who asks, receives and he who seeks shall find and to him who knocks the door shall be opened."

What I am saying is that God expects you to have faith, faith that when you get on your knees in prayer asking Him for His guidance and favor with a new employer, that when you DO go to seek and find, that He shall open the doors for you. But rest assured He would not hold a position open for you forever. If you want to sit around and wait that is fine with Him, but don't get mad at God if when you finally do decide to go look, if that perfect job that He had waiting for you is no longer there.

Imagine for instance when God called Billy Graham to step forward and spread His word if Billy said, "Ahh God not right now ok, I'm really tired after my last job and just want to rest for now". "Sure Billy you go right ahead and rest".

Do you think God would have waited until Billy felt ready? No, He would just move on and found someone else to do the job.

Now, I have to tell you folks that as I write this I feel VERY CONVICTED; you see God told me three years ago to write this book, but quite honestly I didn't feel worthy. It wasn't that I was lazy; I just didn't feel qualified to do the job. Now when I told my wife what God wanted me to do she was all for it. Gosh if God wasn't enough of an endorsement, you would thing a rousing endorsement from my wife would have pushed me into picking up the pen. But instead I let self doubt creep in, one of Satan's favorite tools, "oh Kelly you've GOT TO BE MISTAKEN, God couldn't have meant for YOU to write A BOOK. You've never written anything but some silly old poems and a couple of songs when you were knee high to a grasshopper. A published writer you aren't chump". I mean come on, of course your wife is going to be supportive, she doesn't want to hurt your feelings, but hey I'll tell you the truth. Yea, just put that out of your mind and save yourself the embarrassment, gosh if anything save GOD the embarrassment".

You see if Satan can get you to doubt yourself, especially when it comes to stepping out for God, he wins the battle, and you end of feeling like you've lost the war.

Well Satan was wrong, I can't tell you exactly why God wanted ME to write this or even why my wife truly feels I'm am qualified except that they obviously see something in me that I can not see, something in me that says I am or that I can. Again, you have to have faith in your partner and her walk with Christ, especially in the times when you are not at your strongest, to look for a different kind of wisdom, a woman's wisdom born of her strength in God and her belief in you. So you see there was no difference in my friend who sat around "looking" for a new job. Unless your faith is used to STEP OUT and walk by putting one foot in front of the other, or one word after the other, then what God has planned for you can never come to fruition because you've allowed Satan to sit you on your laurels believing in your "blind faith" that in the end proved to be not faith at all, but was really just a case of laziness. Want respect in your marriage, be willing to work for it, and even more important, be willing to earn it.

Chapter Five

Thanksgiving or The Bedroom

When I first started writing this I pictured God wanting a book strictly about how one is to "Romance His Lady". But I have to admit, and ask God for His forgiveness that it was still based somewhat off my worldly views. Praise God as I looked more and more to Him and asked that only He guide my words and wisdom, that so very much more of Him than I came out.

Don't get me wrong, I believe and try VERY hard to live up to everything you have read and will read, BUT I too am a sinner and am only human, and there are times I'm sure my wife wonders when this "Romantic Guy" she knows so well and loves is going to come roaring back and take back over the body of this raving lunatic she sometimes has the displeasure of seeing. Hey, I'm not happy about that part, I just do everything I can to keep my "worldly" self on the shelf and allow the loving spirit of His grace guide me in everything I say and do.

When God started to speak to me about this chapter it's funny but one of the analogies He gave me was about Thanksgiving dinner. You see I love, and of course He knows it, a BIG Thanksgiving dinner.

A big turkey, sausage and onion stuffing, garlic mashed potatoes (with just a slight hint of horseradish), corn sautéed in butter, cranberry sauce and some of my wife's famous homemade buns! Then for dessert I love to make Pumpkin Pie Cheesecake (weighs in at about 7 pounds), while my wife makes me my favorite homemade Pumpkin Pie, Apple Pie and if I'm lucky, cherry pie. Hey, you can NEVER have enough desserts I always say!

So God says to me, "imagine having your dinner without the stuffing (I LOVE STUFFING), or without the cranberry sauce or rolls. Better yet imagine having Thanksgiving without the main course and you just had dessert".

Now I know some of you are licking your lips, (especially our friends who have been over to one of our dinners) and rubbing your bellies saying, "that's all right with me"; but quite honestly the dinner wouldn't be complete. Guys you wouldn't have been able to have those great leftover Turkey sandwiches with the hot gravy poured over them while watching your games.

Or my wife's favorite turkey, stuffing and cranberry sauce sandwiches (she even got me to try one and I have to say I'm hooked!).

Let's face it though guys, without all the ingredients, all those delicious different plates of mouth-watering recipes, Thanksgiving just wouldn't be complete!

Well, it's no different with romance. If you go straight to the candlelight dinner without the necessary, and **wanted** I might say, nurturing and loving up to your bride, in the end all she will feel she has gotten is some half backed, half put together dinner that was definitely missing all the key ingredients; instead of the romantic, intimate atmosphere that a woman yearns for with her husband. And guys I'm not talking about whispering sweet nothings in her ear. But if you want to go down that road then fine, let's look at from her standpoint in bed. It's like you both go to the same bed and 5 minutes later your done and she definitely knows all she did get was sweet nothings. That guy's is sex, NOT making love to your wife; the lady God prepared just for you. HIS DAUGHTER.

True, intimate, sensual, sexual love, the kind that God, yes God created is making sure she's known all day long that you've been thinking about her, desiring to be with her body *and* soul. Knowing that when you get home from work, your work may be over but you understand that your true job has just begun. Helping her out around the house, or giving her some free time by taking care of the kids so she can do those things she wanted to get done, in or out of the house, that she just couldn't during the day. Then, no matter whether it's a date night or not, getting your sweaty, smelly body into a shower before you lay down with her.

And then Guys, when you start to whisper in her ear, don't make it sweet nothings, but tell her how much you love her, how much she means to you and how great it feels to have her near you. Then YOU proceed to make love to every inch of her body, not as one who is with some unnamed girl you just picked up at the corner bar, but the very essence of your life. The very expression of beauty and wonderment planted within the heart, mind and soul of your being as a young man, only to be placed before you, wrapped by the creator Himself as a precious present for the son He loves, "here my son, a gift from me to you, my daughter, isn't she lovely beyond compare!"

Believe me guys, if you don't approach your bride like this now, start immediately, I guarantee you won't ever have to worry about your own physical pleasure, not only will it come naturally, but she will make sure of it!

This sir is true intimacy with the lady of your life, not your broad, chick or old lady, but your precious present, your bride!

Bottom—line guys are you want to "ROCK HER WORLD", not just her body and her world is a lot more than just the bedroom!

Chapter Six

What Do You Mean "You Forgot?"

One of the hardest concepts for a man to understand about a woman is their uncanny ability to remember EVERYTHING. We guys can get into a small "discussion" with our wives in the morning, come home that night, eat dinner, and then when we turn in expect our wives to make love; then get mad when our wives aren't in the mood.

"What do you mean your not in the mood, you have a headache". "How come?"

"Well Honey maybe you've forgotten this morning but I sure haven't!"

"This morning you say, you mean that little argument we had over who knows what?"

Guess what guys, "the who", is she. Woman carry things, especially hurt feelings until they feel you have recognized and apologized for those hurt feelings, and understand why it is they are hurt to begin with and if you think differently I hope you like cold showers!

Now don't get me wrong, both women and men should never use sex as a tool to get what you want from your mate. Even God refers to this in 1 Corinthians 7:3-5,

" Let the husband render unto the wife due benevolence: and likewise the wife unto the husband." The wife hath not power of her own body, but the husband; and likewise also the husband hath not power of his own body, but the wife. Defraud ye not one the other, except with consent for a time, that ye may give yourselves to fasting and praying; and come together again, that Satan temp you not for your incontinency.

In other words don't use yourselves as tools to get what you want from the other. As God pointed out Satan will use that as a tool against you both.

Now I'm sure some of you are probably saying, "what do you mean I don't have power over my own body, of course I do! No you don't! Not if you entered into a marriage covenant with your partner before and under God. His word say in Ephesians 5:31;

*"For this cause shall a man leave his father and mother, and shall be joined unto his wife, and the two shall become **ONE** flesh." (Boldness mine to emphasize)*

Now getting back to that little argument you forgot all about, even God recognizes and tells us that we be far better off than dealing with a hurt or angry woman. In Proverbs 21:9 He says,

"It is better to dwell in a corner of the rooftop, than with a brawling woman in a wide house".

He also points out further in this same chapter under verse 19:

" It is better to dwell in the wilderness, than with a contentious and angry woman."

So before you expect the ice to melt in the bedroom you better make sure you recognize not only how she feels, but why.

One time my wife and I got into this HUGE fight. It was at bedtime and we broke the first rule of discussion, we were having this discussion in be, guys this is the wrong place to be having any kind of discussion other than asking her how she would like to be pleased sexually, anyhow there are two things I remember about that argument:

First, I was right (yea you say), but in the few times of our life we may actually be right guys, this was one of them. Well Amy went running out of the room and I could tell she was quite upset. I lay there thinking to myself how right I was; meanwhile I heard her weeping in the family room. Just then I heard the Lord say, "Kelly can I ask you a question"? Ok first off I knew He really wasn't asking my permission to ask me a question, but my response was, "ahh God do you have to, I was right?"

"Kelly, what difference does it make"!

"But God I was right!" "I'm hardly ever right, can't I relish this for just a moment at least"? We can be so selfish when we want to be!

"Kelly what matters here, your love or...don't say anything more my Lord, I know what matters"

I then proceeded into the family room and got on my knees in front of my weeping bride and asked her if she could possibly forgive me, for I allowed the subject of the argument to get in the way of the true thing that only mattered, which was my undying love for her.

That in the end it didn't matter who was right or wrong over the topic matter, but that our love was all that did matter because truth of it all, when it all boils down and all things are said and down, two or three weeks down the line neither will really remember the basis of the argument, we will only remember how each handled the outcome.

You see in the reality of life as well as in your relationship, it doesn't matter in the end who was right and who was wrong, especially, if it's that very concept that is stopping you from solving the problem to begin with.

Although it may be hard to understand the concept of asking to be forgiven for something you feel you may have been right about, if you put your pride aside and become the man God has intended you to be and be the first to ask for forgiveness for allowing anything to get in the way of your love for her, you will in the end be far better off than if you allow this thing that has come in between you to fester and grow.

In the end when you have tossed aside what is usually the biggest roadblock in an argument; pride; it allows you to get to the root of the problem and solve it as two people in love. Not two opponents battling for their own cause. Fighting for what they believe are their own injustices. The true injustice of it all is that you allowed something to get in the way of your love for each other, to place potholes in the road of life together, that eventually Satan makes sure you go back over and over and each time the holes get deeper and deeper until one day, your love is swallowed whole.

All because you fought it separately as prideful beings, each fighter in their separate corners of the ring, rather than as tow creatures of Christ brought together by Him as one loving being.

A lot of people believe in the old scripture, An eye for an eye, a tooth for a tooth, but if you look at what Jesus says in Matthew 5:38-39 you get a whole different perspective;

"Ye have heard that it hath been said, An eye for and eye, and a tooth for a tooth: But I say unto you, That you resist not evil; but whosoever shall smite thee on thy right cheek, turn to him the other also".

Now you might say, what does he mean, I'm supposed to let someone beat me to death?

No, Jesus knew that if you were always trying to get even with someone, that the very underlying motive for this is your pride, one of the biggest sins and one of the most vicious traits that can kill not only a romance, but your marriage as well. Jesus also goes on to say in Matthew 7:1-5,

"Judge not, that ye be judged, for what judgment ye judge, ye shall be judged: and with what measure ye use, it shall be measure back to you. And why beholdest thou mote that is in thy brothers eye (or sisters, paraphrasing), but considerest not the beam that is in thine own eye? Or how will thou say to thy brother, Let me pull out the mote out of thine eye; and behold, a beam is in thine own eye?"

In plain English: *before* you judge someone (like your spouse) or cast blame on someone else, you better take a good long hard look in the mirror my friend and see that you are completely blameless, not only in this one argument, but completely, otherwise you are nothing more than a hypocrite.

In John 8 a bunch of townsfolk bring to Jesus a woman who was caught in an adulterous affair, wanting to stone her to death. Jesus then tells the townsfolk in verse 7,

"He that is without sin among you, let him cast the first stone at her. It goes on to say; And they that heard it being convicted by their own conscience, went out one by one, beginning at the eldest, even unto the last; and Jesus was left alone, and the woman was standing in the midst. When Jesus lifted himself up, and saw none but the woman, he said unto her, "Woman where are those thine accusers? Hath no man condemned thee?

SHE SAID, "No one Lord.' And Jesus said to her, "Neither do I condemn you, go, and sin no more."

Men, if you really want your relationship to flourish as Jesus does, then do not only be slow to blame, but be first in the asking of forgiveness for allowing anything or anyone to come in between you and your love for your bride.

"Therefore what God has joined together, let no man sever." Matthew 19:6

Chapter Seven

So you want to get Romantic

Ok, so you've got the basics down in what it takes to establish a romantic mood; so lets talk about the setting. Obviously the setting can be as varied as the individual creating it, but let's say for the sake of argument that this is not exactly your area of expertise, or that you would like a fresh perspective on some new ways to "set the tone". One thing to keep in mind is to not let the weather dictate your pick of settings.

WHAT you say! Let me explain.

One of my wife's favorite romantic dates was on her 25th birthday. I told her we were going to go for a walk on our favorite pier (in our hometown is a beach called Charlotte and it has a pier that extends out about a ¼ of a mile into Lake Ontario), and then we would go to a nice restaurant and have a quiet candlelight dinner. What she didn't know was all that day I had spent setting up that beach to be a romantic getaway. On the boardwalk right on the beach are several nice gazebos. One of them was to be my little booth of romance. Now guys let me tell you something right now, it's the same thing that was told to me as a kid growing up and the same thing I tell my son; if you are going to do something, then do it right, all the way, or don't do it at all. This is no truer then when it comes to making an occasion like your wife's birthday even more special. Women are very detail oriented and they know that generally speaking, men are not. So the first impression you make on her will be the amount of ATTENTION to detail you have made in making sure her "special" time would be even more special; this will end up staying with her for life. A woman notices how much effort their man puts into something, the more effort that is apparent the happier they will be, because in their eyes it tells them you cared enough to try your very best. You see guys it is NOT the amount of money you have spent, but how much of you went into the gift that really counts.

Some men have the hardest time with going out and buying their bride a gift and instead give them cash, trying to hide behind the excuse, she'd be happier with being able to pick something out herself. WRONG! You can buy your wife what may be an absolutely terrible gift, something she would never have brought herself, but if you were to give it to her with an excitement and an attitude worthy of a young child who just spent his only 25 cents to buy his mom the best thing he could, guys your lady is going to be more touched by your true effort in wanting to please her than she would if you gave her $100 and said here, go get whatever. Now I'm not saying she will LOVE the gift guys, just the giver!

Back to the beach:

This gazebo was set up quite perfect for what I had in mind; it had benches that went all the way around. So I set up a table (card table) with a nice lace tablecloth with matching place settings. I used our finest dishes and crystal glasses and water goblets and for the centerpiece I had brought her a beautiful crystal vase and put 25 long stem roses, one for each year of her life. I also had glass-covered hurricane lamps so we could eat by candlelight.

Within the crystal goblet I folded the cloth napkin so that it looked like a large red chrysanthemum. It's actually quite easy to do; you can go to the library or your local bookstore and pick up a book on centerpieces and place settings.

The table setting rivaled that of any 5 star restaurant, I wanted nothing to be left out.

For the dinner I made steamed lobster, grilled rib eye (yes I brought my own grill), baked potatoes with all the fixings, grilled corn on the cob and fresh bread. For dessert I made her a homemade Cherry Cheesecake (something I will say she says I'm great at) with whipped topping.

Ok, so how did I pull this all off you may wonder. First I drove all the supplies there in the afternoon and set everything up. Then about and hour and a half before I was to pick her up I had my brother (God bless him!) and his girlfriend come and keep an eye on everything for me, with instructions to light the fire at a specific time. I then went and cleaned up myself and then proceeded to pick up my bride. After I picked Amy up we headed to what she thought was going to be a short walk on the pier. As we came toward the beginning of the pier where it stretchers out over the water, my bride remarked how something smelled "great"! Just as she was going to start heading out over the pier I turned her to start going up the boardwalk toward the gazebo. Just as I did this Amy looked at me as if to start to say where are we going when she saw the gazebo and it's set up out the corner of her eye. She then looked about 20ft away from where the gazebo was to notice my brother standing there. The look on her face when she saw how decked out this gazebo was and realizing it was all for her was worth a billion dollars. That, gentlemen is what I am talking about. That look that you get when she realizes just how much trouble (though it really is not trouble at all for the one you love) you went through just for her! My brother then walked over and said his goodbyes, gave me a hug and said, "brother you're a class act".

His girlfriend then said pay attention Greg, when do I get something like this!

Throughout that evening and well into the night there were countless couples strolling by the boardwalk, which quite honestly we were quite impervious to, except for what seemed like several times where a girl would hit her boyfriend or husband on the arm and say, "when are you going to do that for me huh"? One time I had to laugh because one gentleman who was the recipient of that particular comment looked at me and said, thanks a lot guy, see what you started"! Now she is gong to expect me to do something like this".

I pray I did and I pray HE did. You see that's what this book, my ministry and my life are all about. Telling men that God wants them to live up to His standard of husbandry, to His level of being a man. To LOVE on your wife, or show the respect to your girlfriend by honoring her with your celibacy and waiting until you marry her, to share the kind of intimacy that God only intended for a marriage. Can I say I did? Not by a long shot.

I truly in my heart and soul wish I had. But that's a topic for another chapter, even maybe another book, titled Pure in Thought.

Anyway, though my brother thought it was a class act and though there were many woman that night who thought the same, I wasn't and don't do what I do for my wife to ever impress other people. I do it to show the absolute love and adoration I have for my precious present, for the daughter that Christ has given only to me and I thank Him for it.

Oh and one the best parts of that day was at night when a huge electrical storm rolled in over the water. Lightening flashes arching over the sky, it was a spectacular show the made us both feel as if God was orchestrating it just for our enjoyment. I put on some romantic music and we slow danced as we watched the show. So you see guys, weather does not have to be a factor!

Understand men that I am not saying that you need to do this every night of the week but your wife should expect to be pampered on a regular basis. It doesn't matter how many children you have (did I mention we have seven, you can at LEAST once a month (I recommend a weekly ritual), say on a Fri night which is when my wife and I normally try to do this) put the kids to bed for her, and then while she is sitting in a nice hot tub that you have drawn for her, Guys, can you say Calgon, YOU proceed to make her an excellent dinner by candlelight.

Normally we try to do this at the table or making up a table right by the fireplace, but I will admit that there have been times that due strictly to exhaustion on both our parts, that we simply share a dinner sitting in our living room while watching a funny, or romantic movie. That's right guys, a romantic movie! But whatever the flavor of the night, we make sure we do it together, without the children around, and in a manner that is pleasing to both. Now I'm going to share something with you that allot of parents will have a hard time believing, we also make it a point to take our children out for a nice and romantic dinner. WHAT you say?! Exactly, if your children don't see Mom and Dad loving on each other some place other than the home, my son won't know this is how he should treat his bride, or my daughters won't know that this is how they should expect to be treated. It's important that children see the love their parents have for each other both in private at home and in public, so they know what God expects of them when they grow up. So that as they get older they understand it isn't all about sex, but the love you show each other outside the bedroom that truly makes a marriage.

It's also important for my son to be taught things like knowing to open the door for a lady (which he does all the time and woman think he's adorable and well mannered for doing it), or to help seat a lady. I can hear the whines and moaning now, "seat a lady, open the door, come on, chivalry is dead"! No guys it isn't, it's just asleep and if we don't wake it up soon and show our young men what the true meaning of being a man is, then we cannot complain when they have children and abandon them. When they beat their wives and become alcoholics. When they become a menace to society and wind up dead or in jail. NO, we won't be able to look them in the eye on visiting day and say why son, and then be shocked when they look back at us and say, well you never taught me different, I was just trying to imitate you Dad.

Wake up guys, our children are dying, our sons are being carted off to jail and to the morgue because we've let chivalry die, because we have let the word Godly Man become a cursing term instead of a loving term. It's time to wake up and show up! It's time to let our sons see us loving, respecting and honoring the ladies we say we love.

If you can't love God how can you love your wife? If you can't love your wife how can you love your children? It may seem to you that I got off the subject of this chapter but the truth is, if you can pay attention to detail for your wife out of love, chances are you'll show that same attention to detail when your loving on your children.

I know I for one, as a father of five drop dead gorgeous daughters, will always make sure my daughters know that unless the guy in her life is an on-fire, totally committed, God fearing, Jesus believing, complete and total gentleman; one who knows her first love will always be her Lord and Savoir; and will have nothing but the total respect and honor for her that she deserves, don't even bother wasting your time. For as I tell them, and will always tell them, "he ladies, isn't worth it"!

Getting back to the romantic side of the house, and speaking of Calgon, another nice thing you can do for your lady is after drawing her that bath, lighting up the room with some scented candles, sprinkle some rose petals over the floor, and then as she is relaxing, cut up a bunch of fruit and cheese and put these on a nice cutting board, along with some chilled fruit juice or her favorite hot beverage and join her. I'll leave the rest up to you. Another simple and cost free night would be to take her for a hike through the nearest park, or if you are lucky enough to live in a place like upstate NY or the Evergreen state of Washington, take her on a hike through a National Forest or even up into the hills overlooking the valley below, just holding hands and talking about your dreams and plans. Your woman wants to know what you dream! You can pack a small picnic and then watch the sun go down with your arm around her or letting her lay her head on your lap, softly stroking her hair. Not only does it make you slow down and appreciate the beauty of God's precious presents, but also it reaffirms in her your commitment to making her second in your life.

Now I know that statement caused a lot of hairs to stand. But it's true, I did say second. God must ALWAYS be first in your life. If you keep Him first He will always provide whatever you need to make her feel like she is always number one. There is nothing on earth my wife knows I wouldn't do for her EXCEPT give up making God number one in my life. But I praise God for giving her the knowledge to know that it is because of Him that I am who I am and without Him, I would be but another man looking to the world for advice, advice not worthy to follow.

And that is all a part about being romantic!

Chapter Eight
Being a Godly Father

There are countless ways you can make just about any situation "special" or romantic while you are together; with or without out your children. One thing that will always make your bride know how much you love her is to love her children, whether or not they're your own flesh-n-blood. Obviously if they are yours it should go without saying that your love should be automatic, though in today's world that statement sadly lacks truth, but when they are not yours that can sometimes be a challenge; and there is nothing that can kill a romance as well as your relationship than to not get along and genuinely love her children. I remember when my wife and I were dating a comment that she made about how happy it made her to see how much I truly cared for and loved her children. She has a son and a daughter from her previous relationship before God brought us together and there is nothing I haven't or wouldn't do for my two children. I have adopted her daughter and will be adopting our son as well for it is as important to me, as well as it is to her, to make sure the children know they are as much a part of our family as the five children we have had together. So whether you have children together or one or both partners bring children into the marriage, make sure gentlemen

that there is no doubt in her mind how important and how much you love them, for to love them is to love her.

There are several times in the Bible where God gives instructions to Fathers in what and how He expects you to view and raise your children. In Ephesians 6:4 He says,

"And, thy Fathers, provoke not your children to wrath; but bring them up in the nurture and admonition of the Lord."

In Psalms 127:3-5; He says,

"Lo, children are an heritage of the Lord: and the fruit of the womb is his reward. As arrows are in the hand of a mighty man; so are the children of youth. Happy is the man that hath his quiver full of them."

In Proverbs 17:6 He states;

"and the glory of children are their fathers".

He also points out that He expects us to raise our children in a godly manner and if you do you can expect to have children who are not only at peace with themselves but also with their parents. In Isaiah 54:13 He proves this by saying,

"And all the children shall be taught of the Lord; and great shall be the peace of they children."

Teach them God also goes on to say in Proverbs 22:6,

"Train up a child in the way he should go; and when he is old he will not depart from it."

Now I cannot and will not say that just because you try to raise your child in a godly manner that they will ALWAYS be "little angles". On the contrary, remember Satan is out to destroy you and your family and the first place he'll usually start is with the one who is most vulnerable, your children. They are more susceptible to temptation and easily drawn into the wrong crowd. Now there are a lot of Christian parents who will say, well my child has the strength to withstand the devil and it would be good for him or her to be around those sinners. Keep in mind parents, even God says in 1Corinthians 15:33,

"Be not deceived; "bad company corrupts good character".

So you must do everything you can to equip them by feeding them the word every chance you get. By equipping your children with the knowledge of God you are empowering them to stand up for what they know to be right, by giving them a firm foundation from which to draw their strength and discern right from wrong when confronted by Satan and his thugs. Equipping them to know how to defend the faith that they have. Equipping them to know how to walk away from the peer pressure when presented with a cigarette, or alcohol, sex or drugs. Without the proper education and the proper equipping they are left to their own understanding, which usually has been peppered with TV ads, school and every other media source available to man and very little of Dad and Mom. Make sure Dad that it is you who they remember more of!

That's why it's important men to start teaching your sons at a young age how to treat the young girls around them, as well as more mature women with respect and honor so that as they grow old they will know to treat the women they court, and eventually their wives, with the honor, respect and love God says they deserve.

One of the ways I use to teach my children not only about God's word, but His wisdom, is to do devotions out of a devotional that caters to children/teens. Afterwards we read a chapter out of Psalms and one out of Proverbs coinciding with the date of the month. For Psalms we just continue until the end and then start over. I figure it can't hurt rereading these two books over and over again. I hope to one-day get them to the point they know them by heart. What better wisdom can one give his child!

Guys another way your child knows they count is by turning off the TV and playing with them. Be it a board game of just a game of catch. Time is what matters the most to them, not necessarily what is occurring during it, as long as the focus is on them! Yea, I know, you've heard all this before, then why aren't you doing it? Being a Rocket Scientist is important to your child, being a father who spends time with them and loves on them is.

Chapter Nine

Why Jesus?

There are many who will read this and ask, "Do I really need Jesus in my heart just to be romantic"? Honestly the answer is no, you don't. However as I said earlier, there is a difference between being and doing. It is even more important when you're considering who your mate is going to be. Before I got to know exactly who God was and where His son fit into my life I was married for 10 years.

To be quite honest with you it was the marriage from hell. Now please don't get me wrong, I am NOT going to tell you how bad my ex-wife was or how everything was her fault. The real truth is if we had both known the Lord we not only would never had met, but quite frankly, we never would have married. Now there are some who would say that only God can bring two people together into a marriage, but you are extremely wrong. God has given us a free will to make our own choices. However I can tell you that without putting your trust in Him and going before Him before making ANY decision, we will always have the tendency to put self first, which in the end we normally find out we didn't exactly make the right decision.

When you seek His will and strive to make His plan your life, you cannot go wrong. You see God ONLY wants His very best for us. But left to our own accord, as my ex and I were at the time, we both ultimately made the wrong choice. It wasn't that we weren't both good people, each with compassionate hearts, but we were both sinners and carried that sin into the marriage. Satan had a hold on both our lives and used this foothold to destroy us both. His hold on me was devastating and led me down paths that no Godly man would ever have taken. I failed God, my wife, my children and ultimately myself by not seeking God as my foundation. Yes, I know it takes two to tangle and I won't say she had no faults, but like I said I'm not here to bash my ex, just to try to explain to you, that as the head of the household, it is YOUR responsibility to be the leader that God has called you to be.

Without God in our lives, she not only did not have the Godly vision that He would have put in her heart, but I didn't have a clue what being a real man was all about. I tried to be what she wanted me to be, but without her own grounding in God's word, her vision was whatever Satan and the world planted within her. Satan used our weakness to throw strife and confusion into our marriage, of which eventually broke down the sandy foundation of which our marriage was built on to begin with.

In 1 Corinthians 14:33 it says,

"For God is not the author of confusion, but of peace, as in all churches."

The NIV translates this as,

"For God is not a God of disorder, but of peace."

If we had had God in our lives to begin with, we would have been patiently waiting for our Lord to supply His will for our lives. We would not have been seeking solace with one another, of which neither of us was properly equipped to supply that which we both needed. Instead we found anger, hurt, confusion and ultimately destruction in the end.

Instead of being washed in His love and then coming together to complete His loving will for two people to spend their lives under His covenant, we instead looked to each other to fill a huge void we each had, a task no two people will ever be able to do. For we will always have a tendency to fail not only ourselves, but our spouses as well when we look to each other for all the answers. And in the end we feel hurt and rejected and even more unfulfilled because our spouse didn't meet our unobtainable expectations. It is completely unfair for either of you to expect your spouse to fulfill you. No one human being can do that and you just set yourself up for failure when the person doesn't meet all your needs. Only God can truly fulfill us and unless you understand going into a marriage you've already set it up to fail.

Will your life and your marriage be strife free because it is based on God, no, not at all. But at least when Satan comes against either of you, you have the Rock to stand on, and you have each other to cover your marriage with prayer. Let me tell you, there is nothing more intimate than getting on your knees together, just you and your bride, prostrating yourself before God the Father in prayer. Lifting one another up and asking for His grace to be sufficient in your hard times. This is what makes marriages stronger, mightier in battle, for as He states in Matthew 18:19-20,

"Again I say unto you, that if two of you shall agree on earth as touching anything that they shall ask, it shall be done for them of my Father which is in heaven. For where two or more are gathered together in my name, there I am in the midst of them."

I told you in the beginning of this book that when your wife is grounded in the word of the God, He would plant a vision of her man within her. However, without God, her vision will be distorted and when you fall short of this vision, which quite frankly you always will because it will always be changing within her, your marriage will falter, as you try to constantly change chasing this "dream guy" of hers. And guys don't try to fool yourself, we all try to change to make the lady in our life happy, but the more you try to chase the ever changing vision, the more you will be lost and in the end, end up hating her because you no longer know who you really are.

But with being grounded in Jesus and constantly seeking Him in your life and His will for your marriage, you will also find yourself changing, only this time the two visions will be more intertwined, thus you are happy seeking His will and she is happy because she sees the great Godly man you are striving to be.

You say you believe in God but your spouse doesn't, that's ok. If at least one of you is grounded in Christ you can cover your spouse and your relationship. Just continue to lift your partner and your marriage up to Him. Pray for His seed to be planted firmly within your spouse and as you seek a stronger relationship with Him and they see the changes within you, it will cause them to want that same "light" they see radiating from you. Be the light and they will seek!

Now fast-forward five years and to a man who has made Jesus the center of his life. Now I am blessed to have the most beautiful woman in the world love me completely and unconditionally just as my Lord who had sent her. There can be NO comparison between my first marriage, which was Godless, and my second, which was founded and built on the Rock. It is like the parable that Jesus speaks about in Matthew 7:24-27,

"Therefore whoever hears these sayings of Mine, and does them, I will

liken him to a wise man who has built his house on the rock: "and the rain descended, the floods came, and the winds blew and beat on the house; and it did not fall, for it was founded on the rock. But everyone who hears these sayings of Mine and does not do them, will be like a foolish man who built his house on the sand; "and the rain descended, the floods came, and the winds blew and beat that house and it fell".

And great was its fall!

My first marriage was built on sand and in the end the fall was great, not only for her and I, but our two sons who were hurt the most. So I implore you to seek God out in your life, ask Him to forgive you for your sins, to be washed pure by the blood of Jesus, and to have His Son, Jesus Christ fill your heart and to be filled by His Holy Spirit. Tell Him that you want His will and only His will for your life and your marriage. If you are not married yet, ask Him to bring the lady He wants to be in your life, if you are already married it is not too late to turn your marriage over to Him. Decide to do it today! Decide to start building a new foundation on the ROCK!

Chapter Ten
Showing Her You C.A.R.E

C.A.R.E –

Constantly Assessing and Removing Ego!

Showing that you care romantically usually to a guy means giving her flowers or candy or perfume. Again this is the world's view of trying to create a certain atmosphere so that we look good. God however wants you to create, become and maintain a spirit of romance.

So what does God want me to do to create this spirit of care and romance?

You know that pile of clothing you dump on the floor every night when you get into bed; you know the socks and pants and anything else that comes off your body that somehow manages to find a home by your bed until the Mrs. comes along and scoops it up yet, once again cleaning up after her man,

PICK IT UP!

Believe it or not it takes 3.5 seconds to bend over, scoop it up and toss it in the hamper.

If you like you can pretend you're a famous basketball player and going for the game winning two points, but instead of winning the game, you will be winning her heart and gratitude!

Know all those whiskers and hairs that get left behind in the sink after your done getting ready in the morning? Take the 2.5 seconds it takes to rinse them down the drain. She'll love you for it!

In Psalms 86:15 we read about a God who is full of compassion,

"But you, O Lord, are a God full of compassion and grace".

Show your wife a Godly man who also has compassion.

Compassion guys isn't always meant to be in a sexual context. Jesus was always moved by His compassion toward man. In Mathew 9:36 it says;

"But when He saw the multitudes He was moved with compassion for them, because they were weary and scattered."

In today's world it's harder than ever to be a woman. If your wife is a working Mom, not only does she have to put up struggling to make herself known as worthy to work along side man, who is always trying to prove she isn't, but then she has to come home and work even harder trying to prove to you and the kids she can still be a wife and a mother.

Show her some compassion by helping her out.

And if your wife is a stay a home Mom, she has to endure even more with the nagging question of what her role is supposed to be. Not only does she normally feel guilty about staying at home, *especially* if you are having any kind of a financial strain, but she has to put up with most men's attitude of, "hey she gets to stay at home, how much easier do you want life to be".

Wrong guys! There is not a TOUGHER job on the planet than to be a stay at home Mom!

Not only does she feel she has to make sure you are taken care of in the morning, that your clothes are washed and your pants and shirts ironed, but that she has fulfilled this vision that she sees in her head of her husband and all her kids sitting around the breakfast table as a family.

And if that doesn't happen, which is more the norm today in our 21st century, eat on the go ways, then somehow she has failed.

So after she has you set, she now gets to make sure all the kids are ready for school, the house is clean, the laundry is done, the dinner is cooked, the kids are chauffeured around town to all their activities that they are involved with, make sure the little ones get their baths, homework is done and then all the kids are tucked snugly in bed. THEN she gets to make sure you are all set for tomorrow, the menu is planned, any appointments are set and then, to top it all off, climb into bed totally exhausted to hear, "what we aren't going to have sex"?

And this doesn't even include taking the kids to the doctors, dentists, the therapists, every sporting event known to man, taking the laundry to the dry cleaners, going to the bank, the post office or a gazillion other places to take care of business that if it weren't for her, YOU would have to do. And then to really top it all off, getting angry with herself because she just didn't manage to get it all done that day, only to have you, you, the man she married, the one who said he loved her for better or for worse, to come home and complain that SOMETHING didn't get done and THEN to have the AUDACITY to sit in your easy chair and grab the stupid remote! I know, been there, done that…

I praise and thank God I now know the difference between being in a marriage and working at your marriage. Yes, marriage is work, and trying to keep the fire alive takes a LOT of it. But like any successful business that the owner spent years refining, the rewards can be numerous. My wife treats me like a King, and though a part of it is because of her beautiful nature, it also has a great deal with how I treat her.

A while back we were at some friends house and as I was kidding around with her and tickling her, which she HATES, she told me to cut it out or else (you know that phrase), and I remarked, I better watch out or you'll replace me!" The reply I got from our friend made me realize I was still doing something right; her comment was; "I doubt it Kelly from what I hear it would take two men to replace you"! I felt humbled but happy that my wife still talks about me that way to her friends even after five kids (we now have seven!). MY secret; you've been reading it all along, Romancing on the Rock.

If you show her you care, that her feelings mean more to you than your buddies, that she means more than the remote control and the Sunday game, that there truly isn't anything you'd rather do than to spend time with her; then the love you get in return will make you feel and walk like a King!

In Proverbs 12:4 it says,

"An excellent wife is the crown of her husband",

by showing you care you too will make your wife want to be that which people would call, an excellent wife. God tells us that we can measure a man by his "fruit",

"But the root of righteousness yields fruit" Proverbs 12:12.

In Proverbs 13:12 we read,

"A man shall eat well by the fruit of his mouth."

By constantly assessing and removing your ego at the door when you go home at night and instead, putt her wants and need before yours, you will ensure that your marriage yields more fruit than you can handle.

Basing it on the Rock and showing you care are GUARANTEED ways to make sure you reap a plentiful harvest.

Chapter Eleven

130 Ways to Please Your Lady

When I first started this I was going to call this chapter, as well as list, "777 Ways To Please Your Lady", but God had shown me that the one and most truest way to please your lady is by following the Word and the Spirit of Christ. By doing so He will show you more ways to love your bride than I could ever begin to write down. SO instead I will simply give you a few. If you don't like any of these, then look to your friends and other married couples in the church. Seek out someone who you know is a Godly man and ask him for advice. It isn't about how much money you spend, but how much thought and effort went into the gift.

1.   Prepare a bath with Calgon or any other of the nice bath additive you can get from your local body shop, as you put the kids to bed, surrounding the tub with candles and her favorite cheeses and fruits. Then join her.

2.   Pack a picnic of fruits and cheeses (yea I know all this healthy food) and find a high hill overlooking a valley to sit on top of and watch the sun go down.

3.   OR have a picnic on the beach.

4.   OR for the more adventurous, have a picnic while on board a highflying balloon!

5.   Take her to a restaurant where a musician will come to your table and sing a love song to her. You say you don't want to embarrass yourself? Leaving ourselves vulnerable in front of her not only shows her that you are secure in who you are, but also that you would be willing even to embarrass yourself if it meant doing something nice for her.

6.   Take a dinner cruise.

7.   Go for a walk! It doesn't matter if it's on the beach or around the block as long as you are **holding her hand** and **TALKING** with her!

8.   Take her for a canoe ride

9.   In some cities like San Antonio or Venice you can take her for a gondolier ride.

10. Take her to an amusement park, and it doesn't matter how old you are either!

11. Have a scavenger hunt, where it is she you are looking for. She is to leave clues/cards at each place giving you hints of where she may be. Prize – use your own imagination!

12. Have the same hunt except let her be the hunter and you be the hunted. Make your last stop be at a very nice hotel, sitting in a tub with tons of candles and rose petals leading from the elevator, right to your bath (you might need to clear or tell the hotel that you will be more than happy to clean up

after yourself, or just have them leading from your door to the bathroom). As she opens the door let there be little trinket gifts leading to the bathroom with a red rose along side each gift. When she opens the door be standing the in the tub holding a dozen roses with a big ribbon and bow around yourself!

13. On her birthday have a dozen roses, one dozen for each year that either you have both been together, or for the number of years old she is, delivered to her no matter where she may be.

14. Leave I LOVE YOU post it notes all over the house and in the car.

15. Leave a hand made card on her pillow telling her how much you love her.

16. Let her sleep in on Saturday while you get up and take care of the kids. And while you are at it, make her breakfast in bed.

17. Give her some money, say anywhere from $50 — $1000 dollars (any budget can be squeezed once in a while) and tell her to go shopping at her favorite mall. There must be one catch; the money can only be spent on her!

18. Then while she is at the mall, have her paged by a delivery person who has a dozen roses for her.

19. Take her to the nearby park and push her on the swing, while telling each other your dreams and desires.

20. If you live in Rochester, NY, take her to Abbott's Custard down on the beach, and then go for a walk along the pier.

21. Leave an I LOVE YOU note on her windshield at work.

22. Go for a ferry ride.

23. While your lady is standing before you naked, proceed to kiss every inch of her body from the top of her head to the tips of her toes, SLOWLY. She'll tell you what to do next. What? Have a hard time about talking about sex and God in the same sentence, guys GOD CREATED SEX!

24. Go window—shopping with her.

25. Play a board game with her.

26. Listen to her!

27. This one deserves repeating – Listen to her!

28. Take her to Maui. (For those of you who can afford it. Perhaps you can start just saving your change up in a jar; it may take awhile but everything worthy is worth the wait.)

29. Go hiking with her.

30. Take her to her favorite play, even if it is a *musical.*

31. Take her to Toronto.

32. If you live in Seattle, take her for a walk along the beach at Carkeek Park.

33. Stand up in front of all your friends at church and tell them what a blessing she has been to you.

34. Play cards with her.

35. Take her to Victoria Secret and buy her the prettiest nightgown and then tell her you can't wait to see her in it (remember this one is for married folks only, if single you will have to wait).

36. Write a Declaration of your Love to her.

37. Have the Declaration of Love published in the local paper.

38. Write her a love letter and have it mailed to her Certified.

39. If you have one in your city, take her to a revolving restaurant, making sure you have reservations by the window so you can enjoy the view together.

40. Go for a walk in Letchworth State Park in Rochester NY during the fall season. It has some of the most beautiful scenery in the entire country.

41. Open her car door for her. ALL THE TIME! (Yes, even after 14 years I STILL open doors for her!)

42. Take her to FAO Schwartz and let her buy her favorite stuffed animal.

43. Take her on a mini cruise.

44. Take her to the ballet.

45. Go window shopping/site seeing in a small quaint town like Poulsbo Washington.

46. Take her to the pet store and buy her, her favorite animal.

47. Tell her how great she looks. Make this a daily habit!

48. Show up at her work and take her to lunch.

49. If she is a stay at home mom, tell her that a delivery person is coming over so please be dressed respectively and then show up with a babysitter and take her to lunch.

50. If she is a stay at home mom, call her and tell her not to cook dinner, dinner is on you; then make her a great meal with your own hands (no take out guys).

51. Buy, and wear a T—Shirt that says, "SHE IS THE GREATEST!"

52. Go antique shopping with her.

53. Go garage sale hopping with her.

54. Be consistent with helping her around the house.

55. Buy a small gift like a necklace or tennis bracelet and place it in a small box along with a love letter. Then place this in a medium box wrapped in paper that you have written, I LOVE YOU all over. Then place this in yet a larger box, which is wrapped in paper that you have X's and O's along with the words, "TO MY SOUL MATE" written all over.

56. Stick up for her in front of everybody, especially your family! Your family's opinion should NEVER mean more to you than hers. She is your mate, not them!

57. Have lots of pictures of her in your office and make sure she is aware of it.

58. Go for a walk in the park barefoot while it is raining.

59. Pick up after yourself, before being asked.

60. Take her to church, regularly.

61. PRAY WITH HER!

62. Better yet, get naked with her, then get on your knees and pray with her. Why naked. It shows her that you can be completely vulnerable and exposed in front of not only God, but her as well.

63. TURN THE TV OFF!

64. If she wants to go shopping and there is a game on, shut it off and go with her anyway. The game will still go on regardless and then be over, the results meaning nothing to your life; but the results of you going with her will far outlast the time you spent watching that game.

65. Instead of working that extra hour of overtime, go home and spend it with her.

66. Find a gazebo on a lake (one of my favorite spots) and have dinner with her as you both watch the sun go down.

67. Take her to HER favorite restaurant even if you don't like it.

68. Take her to NY to see a Broadway show.

69. Watch some fireworks with her.

70. Then set off your own fireworks, kissing her and holding her

between each volley and telling her how she's the spark in your life.

71. Take her back to the restaurant or place you proposed and get on one knee, only this time tell her how happy you are for the day she said YES.

72. Go out to the car and get the umbrella for her when it's raining so she doesn't have to get her hair all wet after working so hard to make it look nice for you.

73. Acknowledge how great she looks before taking her out or even in the AM before heading off to work.

74. Establish and maintain a meeting night where for at least ½ hour on a weeknight, you set aside time to have a one on one talk. Where you can discuss your week or anything else on your minds.

75. Establish the same as above except include the children in on this session.

76. Have another night, for example Friday night, where after you have given the kids a bath, and put them down for the night, you draw her a bath and while she is soaking, cook her a great meal.

77. Take her for a plane ride over the mountains on a sunny day.

78. Go bike riding with her.

79. Have a monthly date night where she gets to pick the place to go.

80. Rotate nights out, where at least once a month you or her goes out and spend some time with your own friends. Make sure you both agree on time frames so to not cause undue worry.

81. When she is not feeling well, take a sick day and take care of her for a change.

82. Offer to do the grocery shopping for her occasionally.

83. Go grocery shopping with her, <u>without complaining.</u>

84. Share the responsibility of getting the kids to their appointments and weekend games.

85. For Valentines Day try doing something away from the ordinary roses and instead buy her a dozen bouquets of wild flowers, telling her she brings out the wild man in you!

86. Unless it is something she is absolutely crazy about, keep your gift buying on personal holidays like her birthday, to personal items and NOT household items.

87. Unless your handing her $1000 dollars to go to the mall on a NON holiday event, then don't ever give her cash in a card as a gift and tell her to buy whatever she wants. What she wants is for you to take the time and the heart to get her something yourself.

88. Women want, and need validation from their man that they are doing ok by YOUR standards. Reaffirm her!

89. Tell your bride how beautiful you think she is on a constant **daily** basis, not on a quarterly or semi—annual basis.

90. If she does say something that hurts, tell her, don't squash it, ignore it or tuck it away. By being honest and open with her she will not only get to know more about what makes you tick, but respect you and thank you for having the ability to share your feeling with her. It isn't unmanly or un-Godly to share how you feel with the one you love. **COMMUNICATION!**

91. Don't **ever, ever, EVER** compare her to your old girlfriends or ex. As a matter of fact, don't even bring them up and if they do pop up in a conversation be sure to tell her she outshines them all!

92. Remember guys there is a difference between compassionate honesty and brutal honesty. If it lifts her and or the relationship up, that's compassionate honesty. If it hurts her or tears her down, that's brute honesty. God says to always lift one another up. In 1 Thessalonians 5:11 He says, *"Therefore encourage one another and build each other up."*

93. Another one worthy to repeat: Listen to her!

94. Give her a call in the middle of the day just to say I love you.

95. Take the trash out without having to be asked.

96. Take turns getting up in the night to feed the baby, and if she has really had a bad day or isn't feeling well, take all the shifts for her; regardless of how many nights in a row you may have to until she is back on her feet. It is also important that you do it with a cheerful heart and not one of agonizing and complaint.

97. Offer to take the clothes to the laundry mat or some other chore you know she hates.

98. Watch a romantic movie with her occasionally and don't make fun of her if she gets emotional during it.

99. If you are moved by it, don't be afraid to show it in front of her.

100. See your doctor on an annual basis for a check up and routine physical. It shows her you not only care about yourself, but her as well.

101. Exercise with her.

102. If there's a movie she wants to go and see, wait and see it together. If for whatever reason you don't wait, then make sure you are willing to see it a second time with her, without complaining about it.

103. Replace the empty roll of toilet paper. (See 104)

104. Preferably in the direction that SHE likes it to hang.

105. Take the kids out for an ice cream or whatever else without her so that she can have the time alone.

106. Do 105 but this time take her with you.

107. Read the Song of Solomon to her changing all the female references to her name.

108. Be the first to say I'm sorry, even if it isn't your fault.

109. Walk on the left hand side of the road. (Yea, that Chivalry thing again)

110. Open the door for her, always. (And again!)

111. Do not use profanity, especially in front of her. (God calls us to a higher standard, EPH 5:4)

112. Take her to a ball game.

113. Let her do the decorating of the house.

114. Trust her. **Period**.

115. When she's with you, don't be afraid to stop and ask for directions. After all do you want to waste time on manly pride (a sinful thing), or, get to where you are going so you can spend time with her outside of the stresses of traveling?

116. Go for a ride and get lost on the back roads enjoying the scenery and company along the way. (Of course you can bring the GPS along so you can switch it back on when ready to be "found".)

117. When you're at a friend's house for a picnic or dinner, fix her plate for her.

118. Know that favorite tie she loves and you hate, wear it for her.

119. Know that dress that she has wanted that is really outrageously expensive. Splurge and buy it for her anyway. She's worth it.

120. Be sure to tell her the minimum of once a day that you Love her!

121. Don't be afraid to say it in front of other people, especially your male friends.

122. In your prayer together, make sure you thank God for her.

123. If you moved her far from her family, don't gripe about the phone bill.

124. Also be willing to send her home, alone, while you take care of the kids.

125. Amplify her good points. Don't be so quick to point out her bad. If she asks, use tact and grace saying it with love. No, we do not want to ever lie to each other, but remember what God says about lifting each other up.

126. Don't make her the main focal point of where you go to get everything you need in life; take that to God. Only He can fulfill your every need, She is only human.

127. Volunteer to change the baby's diaper, especially the bad ones.

128. Quit drinking. If you need to get drunk, then drink of the new wine. If you don't know what that is, you need GOD!

129. Quit smoking. It stinks and it doesn't make you sexy or cool. Only stinky, she doesn't need that.

130. Care about how you look. Not just for her, but for God as well.

This list can be indefinitely expanded upon and I pray you add your own, just remember one thing, if she doesn't know how much you love her on the inside, what you do on the outside will seem like a simply futile effort of just going through the motions. So try this last one every so often so that you will always be aware of where she is at:

131. Ask her if she knows how much you truly love her. If her answer is no, ask her what you can do to show it and then be willing to do it. Sadly there are so many couples out there that really don't know how they feel toward each other simply because they just assumed the other knew or worse, had the attitude of, "of course she knows I love her, after all I'm with her right?" Wrong! Tell her, write it down, speak it, sing it, recite it, do whatever it takes to get the message across and I don't mean by using ESP! We all know what the word assume means and it's one of the biggest destructive attitudes one can have in a relationship. If those who aren't able to speak can use the gift of sign language and communicate so wonderfully, it should be a piece of cake for those of us who can.

There may be many things on this list that you will say seem pretty simple. Well guys it's the simple things in life that make most woman the happiest. They are not looking for you to whisk them away to Paris every weekend, just to take the time to tell them AND show them that they truly are your love and your life.

The one theme that has been listed here but may not have been given the true importance and the priority that woman give it; the one thing that is the very cheapest thing in terms of your cost, but worth the most in her eyes; is to HOLD HER. Hold her hand in the car, in church, while going for a walk, at the movies. Anywhere you may be, take the time and effort to grab hold of her hand as you go through life together. This, more than anything else you do or say, shows her that you are happy she is a part of your life and you like being with her!

But even more important than this is communicating all the time, no matter what it may be. Work things through. Men don't "stuff it" or you will blow it.

Understand that woman think with their hearts, where as men try to use the logic of their brain. That's what sets woman apart from men, is their ability to reason with their feelings that flow from the heart and not all the complexities that clutter the brain. You've heard many women say they have this woman's intuition; that comes from the filling of the heart, not the mind.

When you allow yourself to think from the heart it allows you to go with decisions that make you feel good, not appear to be good, as the brain would have you think. And don't begin to think that I am saying woman are not intelligent, for they are in some ways far more brilliant than men; they know they have a brain but realize happiness comes most often when you listen to the heart, and not the head.

Men often think they can use their head to figure out their heart, believing that it is the brain that is the most complex organ. The only reason it is the most complex is because we keep thinking about it!

When it comes to dealing with woman, we need to use less brain matter and more heart matter. For to the woman it is the heart of a man that matters most.

Reach to the heart when dealing with a woman and you will find yourself at a new level of understanding when it comes to love.

Chapter Twelve

The Bottom Line

You've heard me talk and use the expression "bottom line", companies too like that phrase. What it boils down to is at the end of the day how profitable you were that day, what was your bottom line. How did you perform on the job, how good was the product you sold or the service that you gave your customer, and even more importantly, how you treated those customers while serving them, will all affect your bottom line.

Now suppose someone came to you and said I can introduce you to this person who can increase your bottom line 30, 60 a hundred fold from where it is now. Your probable response would normally be one of two things:

1. You would either stare at this person in disbelief and walk away or

2. You would jump up and down shouting for joy and maybe throw in a couple of halleluiahs saying bring him on!

Well when it comes to LOVE relationships there is no one better person to bring in and show you how to do it properly than the very creator of Love Himself, God; who by His grace and love gave us His one and only Son, Jesus Christ, to learn to love in the manner that God intended us to do. So by making God as the center of your life, by putting Him as your number one priority, by seeking His will for your life, by placing this at the top of your list in ways to please her, He WILL ALWAYS give you far more ideas of what will work for you, than any man could author.

He says it best in His Word under Mathew 7:24;

"Therefore whosever heareth these sayings of mine, and doeth them, I will liken him unto a wise man, which built his house upon the ROCK"…………..

The End….

To the Ladies:
Crown or Cancer?

An excellent wife is the crown of her husband, but she who causes shame is like rottenness to his bones. Proverbs 12:4 This guide has said a lot to guys in how they should treat, act and speak to their wife, but as we all know it takes two to make a successful relationship. As this Proverb states, if a man has a wife he can count on, one who loves him, trusts him and above all, respects him, a man feels he can take on the world with his partner by his side. But as this Proverb also states, let her be one that causes him shame and it is like rottenness, or put another way, a cancer that eats away at his very soul.

Ladies though most men won't openly admit it, a woman holds vast power over her man. With her words and actions, or lack thereof, she can elevate him to new heights or destroy his very soul. Like a cancer that eats away his bone marrow, thus destroying the very skeleton that holds him up, a woman's treatment of her husband can determine a man's own view of who he really thinks he is. If you don't respect your husband and instead speak to him in a hurtful, disrespectful manner, it is like him being the assistant to the knife thrower in a circus; he standing before the bulls-eye while his wife throws her daggers, but it's actually him who is the true target and she indeed has a deadly aim, never missing the heart of her willful assistant. The truth is a man can go to war and fight deadly foes feeling victorious in battle, blessed he has made it home to his wife, but let him feel his wife does not trust or respect him and he is defeated without a shot ever being fired. If you are the type of woman that tears her man down by words or action, you are in fact, that rottenness God speaks of!

Ladies a man must first feel his wife respects him, that she knows that God has placed him as the head of the home. Just as any CEO/Owner of an organization, or even the Sr. Pastor of a church, the very position itself demands a level of respect; even if you feel you can't respect the person who holds the position. I understand that there are some men who may not act the part of a leader, who has not taken up the mantle God has placed on him, be it all or even some of the time, however, this is NOT your problem or responsibility, but his! He WILL have to answer to God one day about how he headed up his family. I know there are some of you who will say, "Pastor my husband refuses to act like the head of his own body, let alone this family". Again, I tell you, you hold power you know not. If you tell your man that he is the head and that you WILL NOT accept or take on his responsibility as the head whether he likes it or not, MOST men will step up to the plate with enough encouragement, help and yes, some prodding ladies here and there. Cloaked in prayer and humility, eventually he will become that man God has called him to be. For some of you it will be a season fraught with frustration, anger, hurt and confusion, and even at times fighting off the desire to lay "holy hands' on him, but you must remember with God, all things are possible!

For some of you it really is more the matter of your own issues keeping you from trusting your man to be the leader. One of the biggest ones for many of all of us is control issues. Unfortunately for some women, control issues have developed because of hurt and mistrust from previous relationships causing them to put up walls that will keep them from letting go and letting God! Painful experiences we go through in life cause us all to vow to never let them happen again, thus the need to control everything around us. A controlling woman can have as detrimental an effect on a marriage as a man who won't "step up to the plate". A man can never assume his proper role if he has a wife that refuses to give up control over the headship of the home. There have been countless books and millions of hours of therapy that have addressed these issues and tried to find a cure, but it still all comes down to going right back to God's word and He says that we are to *speak to one another in psalms and hymns and spiritual songs, singing and making melodies in your heart to the Lord, giving thanks always for all things to God the Father in the name of our Lord, Jesus Christ, submitting to one another in the fear of God. Eph 5:1-21*

Can you imagine being able to give thanks for all things? That's right, even that hardheaded, un-romantic, TV remote bearing man. Ladies, remember it's your job, and yes, your responsibility according to the covenant you swore on, to love him right where he is at! It's God's job to change him and He's not taking applications for an assistant! Love, respect and prayer. If prayer can move mountains, and God says it can, than God can move your man!

Though I speak with the tongues of men and of angels, but have not love, I have become sounding brass or a clanging cymbal. And though I have the gift of prophecy, and understand all mysteries and all knowledge, and though I have all faith, so that I could remove mountains, but have not love, I am nothing. And though I bestow all my goods to feed the poor, and though I give my body to be burned, but have not love, it profits me nothing. Love suffers long [and] is kind; love does not envy; love does not parade itself, is not puffed up; does not behave rudely, does not seek its own, is not provoked, thinks no evil; does not rejoice in iniquity, but rejoices in the truth; bears all things, believes all things, hopes all things, endures all things. Love never fails. I Cor 13:1-8

This chapter ends by saying; *"And now abide faith, hope, love, these three; but the greatest of these [is] love."*

It takes a ton of faith and hope in both Christ and your man, faith God will hear your prayers and hope your man will obey Him when God speaks to his heart. It will also take patience on your part to both love and respect him as Christ works on him and to have faith that he can in fact, become the man God has called him to be. But, at the end of the day the one thing you will always have control over is whether you decide to be the Crown on his head or the cancer in his bones.

If you chose the latter (and yes, it **IS A CHOICE**), and your relationship does not last, you will never be able to say I gave it my all. After all His word says...

Love never fails...and that is truth above all!

www.ingramcontent.com/pod-product-compliance
Lightning Source LLC
Chambersburg PA
CBHW030358290526
45785CB00004B/1800

* 9 7 8 1 4 5 6 7 1 2 0 4 4 *